KU-626-897

THE OFFICIAL
QUEENS PARK RANGERS
ANNUAL **2022**

Written by Francis Atkinson
and Matt Webb
Designed by Adam Wilsher

A Grange Publication

© 2021. Published by Grange Communications Ltd., Edinburgh,
under licence from Queens Park Rangers. Printed in the EU.

Every effort has been made to ensure the accuracy of information
within this publication but the publishers cannot be held responsible
for any errors or omissions. Views expressed are those of the author
and do not necessarily represent those of the publishers or the
football club. All rights reserved.

Photographs © Rex Features

ISBN 978-1-913578-80-0

CONTENTS

CONTENTS

MANAGER'S *Welcome*

T IS once again my pleasure to write a few words of welcome and thank you for your continued support in the face of an extremely challenging period for us all.

With the season now in full swing, I want to again highlight the significance of the return of our supporters to the stadium.

The 2021/22 campaign has already given us the opportunity to once again savour having our supporters backing the team – both home and away. The passion of genuine fans, the atmosphere you create and the impact it can have on the team is clear for all to see.

Therefore, my first and most obvious welcome is to each and every R's fan – it is great to see you, you have been so sorely missed!

The players worked extremely hard in pre-season and this has been evident with the level of intensity they have already displayed – a factor that will be so important for our league campaign this season.

The squad fully appreciate where they are and what is expected of them, individually and collectively, and that optimism and expectation is one that they've got to feed off. The optimism comes from the fact that they worked so hard last season, finished strongly, delivered good performances and excited the fans.

The end result of that is quite naturally optimism and we have to make sure we respond to that. You can't hide from it –

you have to embrace that expectation. You'd rather be in a team that's expected to do well, expected to kick on.

We can't match the budgets of some of the bigger clubs in the division, that goes without saying, but at the same time we've had continuity in players and staff and that can go a long way to counteracting the spending powers of other clubs.

We've got a responsibility and I hope very much that the players will relish it and hopefully respond to it.

Finally, once again, it is a very sincere welcome back to all of our supporters.

As I repeatedly say, the backing you give the team is always greatly appreciated and never taken for granted.

Come on you R's!

Mark Warburton

7

WELCOME
HOME!

WE MAY have enjoyed an excellent second half of the campaign last season, but it just wasn't the same without you lot.

After nearly a year and a half without capacity crowds in W12, R's fans are finally back at Kiyan Prince Foundation Stadium as we all look to make the the 2021/22 season one to remember – for the right reasons.

THE **NEW** BOYS

Some new and not-so-new faces signed up to the QPR cause over the summer...

JORDY DE WIJS

First through the door on 13th May was the permanent arrival of Dutch centre-half Jordy de Wijs from Hull City. The 26-year-old joins on a three-year deal for an undisclosed fee having previously impressed during a loan stint with the R's in the second half of last term where he scored once in nine appearances.

The player, who began his career at PSV Eindhoven before heading to Hull in July 2018, is now looking forward to continuing his footballing story with the Hoops.

"I'm really pleased that the club have the confidence in me to make the deal permanent," he said. "I can't wait to play many more games for QPR.

"During the second half of the season, we were excellent and overcame many top teams. I think we've shown why we should be fighting at the right end of the table next year."

SAM FIELD

A week later, another loanee from last season made the move permanent in the shape of Sam Field.

The 23-year-old joins on a three-year deal for an undisclosed fee from West Bromwich Albion. Rangers also hold the option of a fourth year.

The central midfielder - who came through the ranks at the Baggies - impressed during 19 appearances in W12 last term, scoring once.

"Sometimes you feel that chapters are up in your life, and I felt it was the right time to move on for good," he said. "I had a feeling in January that if I could get this move right, I could stay here.

"I've enjoyed every moment of my time here so far. We have a great group of lads and the way the end of the season went means we all can't wait to get going again."

CHARLIE AUSTIN

The transfer all QPR fans had been waiting for came on 2nd June when Charlie Austin sealed his return to the club on a two-year deal from West Bromwich Albion.

The popular striker had spent the second half of last season on loan at Kiyan Prince Foundation Stadium, bagging eight times in 19 starts.

The 32-year-old had previously notched 48 goals in 89 games for the R's between 2013-2016.

"I'm really pleased to get it done and to be able to continue my journey here," he said.

"I know this is the right move for me and the right move for my family.

"I was going through a period where I wasn't enjoying my football - I came here and enjoyed it straight away.

"I love everything that the club stands for. It's a family club and one that I'm suited to."

ANDRE DOZZELL

Midfielder Andre Dozzell was the next to arrive, penning a three-year deal on 15th June after signing for an undisclosed fee from Ipswich Town. The club also has a further year's option.

The 22-year-old - son of former Ipswich and Tottenham Hotspur man Jason Dozzell - had been at Portman Road since joining their academy at the age of eight and had made close to 100 appearances for the Tractor Boys.

"I felt now was the right time to take this step in my career," said England youth international Dozzell. "This takes me out of my comfort zone, and I just think it's the right time.

"I was aware they [QPR] were tracking me for quite some time. It's always nice to feel wanted."

JORDAN ARCHER

Goalkeeper Jordan Archer signed on a two-year deal on 7th July after his contract expired at Middlesbrough. The 28-year-old, who came through the ranks at Tottenham Hotspur, has made more than 200 professional appearances to date, the majority of those coming in a four-year stint at Millwall.

After leaving the Lions in 2019, he spent time at Fulham, Motherwell and Boro prior to heading for W12.

"There's a great crop of young goalkeepers here and the club feel I can add experience to the group," said Archer.

"I saw how well Seny Dieng did last season. I'm excited to come in, work with him and I'm sure we can push each other."

SAM McCALLUM

Sam McCallum joined QPR on a season-long loan from Norwich City on 12th July. The 20-year-old left-sided defender signed for the Canaries from Coventry City 18 months ago before being loaned back to the Sky Blues.

He made 41 Championship appearances for Mark Robins' team last term and is now looking forward to spending the 2021/22 campaign with the R's.

"I'm proper excited to get going," he said. "When QPR requested the loan, it was a no brainer. This is a massive club.

"I want to get some game time, but I know I'll have healthy competition here from Lee Wallace.

"I'm fit and ready to go - I just can't wait to get started."

JIMMY DUNNE

Jimmy Dunne became QPR's eighth summer signing when he joined from Burnley for an undisclosed fee on the 13th July.

The defender has agreed a three-year deal with the club having a further 12-month option.

The 23-year-old Irishman came through the academy at Manchester United before joining the Clarets at 18. He went on to make seven first-team appearances with the Lancashire side as well as taking in loan stints at Barrow, Accrington Stanley, Hearts, Sunderland and Fleetwood Town.

"It's a massive step for me," said Dunne. "The loan spells were really good for me but where I'm at now I believe it's important to go on a journey with someone.

"This looks like a really good environment to be part of."

STEFAN JOHANSEN

Stefan Johansen finally joined QPR from Fulham on a permanent basis for an undisclosed fee in late July. The 30-year-old midfielder put pen to paper on a three-year deal.

Johansen spent four months on loan with the R's last season and was a critical part of the side's successful second half to the campaign, which saw Mark Warburton's men rise from 19th in the Championship table to ninth.

"It is great to be back," Johansen said.

"This is a good fit. When the gaffer brought me in last season, I felt the way I play suits the way he wants to play. He has played a big part in making this permanent.

"I come here where there is a good group of players and staff, and I am very much looking forward to it.

"The support of the fans on social media meant a lot. I saw the messages and it means I had a good spell here before – hopefully I can do that again."

MOSES ODUBAJO

Moses Odubajo became summer signing number nine when he joined QPR on a one-year deal.

The club also have a further year's option on the 28-year-old.

Odubajo, out of contract after leaving Sheffield Wednesday at the end of last season, had been training with QPR during pre-season and impressed during that time.

The full-back, who played under R's boss Mark Warburton previously with Brentford, was looking forward to life in W12, saying: "I have got to know the lads really well and it's a manager who I have played with before, so the move just felt right.

"The manager knows what I can do and he knows what I am capable of."

THE NUMBERS:
2020/21

A statistical look at QPR's 2020/21 Sky Bet Championship campaign...

POINTS WON	WINS	DRAWS	LOSSES	GOALS SCORED
68	19	11	16	57

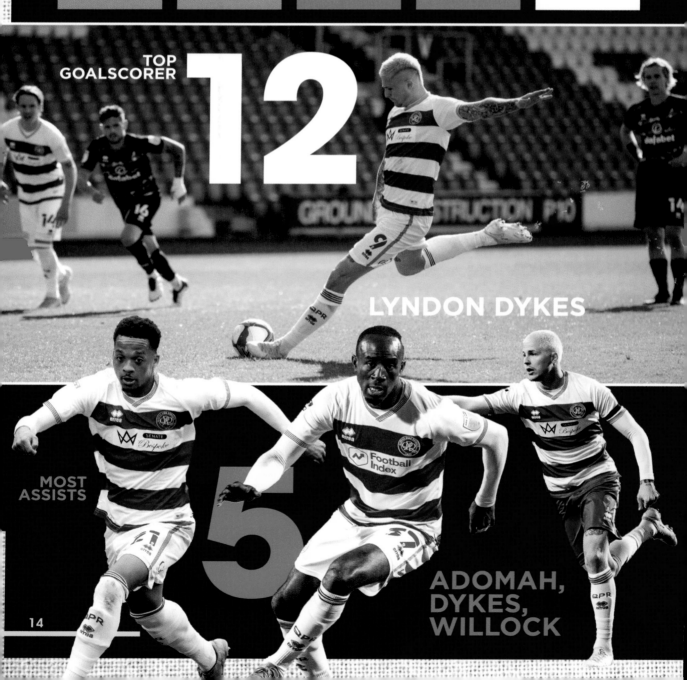

TOP GOALSCORER 12 — LYNDON DYKES

MOST ASSISTS 5 — ADOMAH, DYKES, WILLOCK

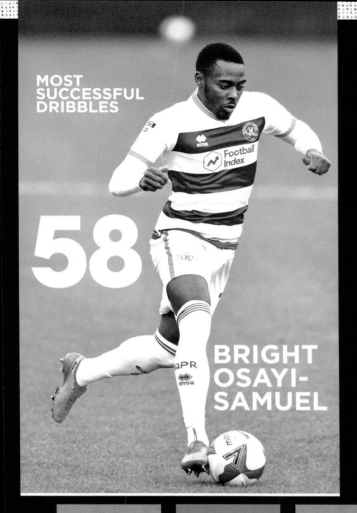

MOST
SUCCESSFUL
DRIBBLES

58

BRIGHT
OSAYI-
SAMUEL

MOST
APPEARANCES

46

YOANN
BARBET

MOST
SUCCESSFUL
PASSES

2,567

YOANN
BARBET

AVG. POSSESSION	GOALS CONCEDED	CLEAN SHEETS	YELLOW CARDS	RED CARDS
52%	**55**	**15**	**79**	**3**

MOST
TACKLES
WON

54

ROB
DICKIE

MOST AERIAL
DUELS WON

212

ROB
DICKIE

LONG LIVE THE PRINCE

TO MARK the 15th anniversary of his tragic death, Kiyan Prince has returned to life as the professional footballer he should have been.

A talented 15-year-old playing for Queens Park Rangers, Kiyan's life was tragically cut short in 2006 when he was stabbed while attempting to break up a fight at his school. Honouring Kiyan, his father Dr. Mark Prince OBE works to inspire and empower vulnerable young people through the Foundation that bears his son's name.

Fulfilling his childhood dream, Kiyan has been officially re-signed by QPR and given the squad number 30, while also being listed as a squad member on all matchday programmes.

Partnering with EA SPORTS, Kiyan has been added to the QPR team roster available in FIFA 21. Fans across the globe can now play as Kiyan in-game. EA SPORTS FIFA developers worked closely with Kiyan's family, friends, former team-mates and coaches to integrate him into the game. From ageing his appearance using images from his teen years, to developing his on-pitch characteristics and style of play - all based on speaking to those closest to him - Kiyan has been developed as the superstar he would've been.

Mark Prince, Kiyan's father, explains: "I want my son to be remembered not for the tragedy of his death but for the triumph of his achievements. Through this campaign my hope is that the world finally gets to glimpse Kiyan's incredible potential fulfilled. We get to honour his talent. And, hopefully, we can inspire other kids to honour their own talent, too - whatever their own strengths might be."

The imagery of Kiyan being used has been developed by Framestore – the special effects studio behind Avengers: Endgame – with input from the Prince family and scientists at the University of Bradford. A combination of advanced AI technology and photo-real illustration was used to virtually recreate Kiyan as the 30-year-old pro footballer he'd be today.

The life of a professional footballer would not be complete without a series of brand endorsements. With the support of adidas, Kiyan will wear the 20/21 adidas COPA boot in FIFA 21 and members of the public will see Kiyan's likeness across some of the UK's most iconic billboards – including Piccadilly Circus and Oxford Street – as part of a JD Sports advertising campaign.

Topps are also introducing Kiyan into their Match Attax game, with a special edition collectable card.

Members of the public who want to support the campaign can donate to the Kiyan Prince Foundation by texting KPF (then the amount) to 70490.

The Foundation's work has seen Kiyan's father Dr. Mark Prince honoured with an OBE and led QPR to rename their ground Kiyan Prince Foundation Stadium.

Les Ferdinand, director of football at QPR, said: "As a club we have worked closely with the Kiyan Prince Foundation and it has been an honour to get to know Mark on a personal level during that time. What he has been through is every parent's worst nightmare and his response to such a tragedy has been truly inspiring.

"When we named our stadium after the Kiyan Prince Foundation in 2019, we invited Mark to the training ground to speak with our players. We felt it was important they understood the history of the Foundation and what it stood for. The squad were truly humbled by Mark's bravery and his dedication to use his pain to prevent others from having to walk the same path he has had to walk.

"We continue to stand shoulder to shoulder with Mark and are delighted to see Kiyan in the QPR squad for the 2021/22 season."

To raise further funds and awareness, the campaign is being supported by a major PR drive across TV, audio and social channels, involving a host of celebrities and influencers under the headline 'Long live the Prince'. For more information, please visit: www.thekpf.com.

James Salmon, marketing director, EA SPORTS FIFA Brand, said: "By adding Kiyan in-game this year, we not only want to celebrate what an incredibly-talented footballer he was and should have been, but also continue to offer EA SPORTS FIFA as a platform to raise awareness of the Kiyan Prince Foundation."

Within FIFA Ultimate Team, players can access custom Kiyan Prince vanity items through the completion of in-game objectives, including a Kiyan Prince Foundation kit inspired by the 2004/05 QPR home kit, and an honorary TIFO of Kiyan that appears every time a goal is scored.

The campaign has been created on a pro-bono basis by ENGINE and all proceeds raised are going directly to the Kiyan Prince Foundation.

LONG LIVE THE PRINCE

19

FOCUS ON...

SENY DIENG

ASHVILLE HOLDINGS

MARRIED: No

CHILDREN: No

CAR: Audi

FAVOURITE TV PROGRAMME: Power

FAVOURITE PLAYER (WORLD FOOTBALL): Paul Pogba

MOST PROMISING TEAM-MATE: Chair, Willock & Dickie!

FAVOURITE 'OTHER' TEAM: Arsenal

CHILDHOOD FOOTBALLING HERO: Ronaldinho

FAVOURITE OTHER SPORT: Basketball

MOST MEMORABLE MATCH: Senegal debut

FAVOURITE MEAL: Some special rice with chicken.

FAVOURITE HOLIDAY DESTINATION: Senegal

FAVOURITE PERSONALITY: Will Smith

FAVOURITE ACTIVITY ON DAY OFF: Relaxing, going for food, shopping.

FAVOURITE MUSICIAN / BAND: Chris Brown, Young Thug, Gunna.

POST-MATCH ROUTINE: Gym workout, eat, relax watch a movie.

BEST FRIEND(S) IN FOOTBALL: Djibril Sow and Ulisses Garcia.

BIGGEST CAREER INFLUENCE: Tony Silva and Steve Mandanda.

PERSONAL AMBITION: Win the Champions League.

IF YOU WEREN'T A FOOTBALLER, WHAT WOULD YOU BE: Boxer

SHEPHERD'S BUSH
SKIPPERS

It takes a certain type of player to captain a side.

Gritty, determined, vocal, encouraging, inspirational, born leader.

Fortunately, QPR have a rich history of first-team skippers. Here are a selection from over the years...

MIKE KEEN

MIKE Keen spent 10 years with the R's, making 393 appearances and netting 39 times between 1959 and 1969.

He was most notably captain of the famous 1967 League Cup-winning side which also won the 1966/67 Third Division championship by 12 points. Keen played at wing-half and was ever present in the QPR line-up from March 1962 to September 1968 – he never missed a game for the boys in blue and white hoops.

Captained by Keen, the R's had burst into life in '66/67 when the team – managed by Alec Stock and also featuring the audacious talents of Rodney Marsh – made a significant impact on English football.

Mike had saved QPR from elimination in the third round of that stirring League Cup campaign when he scored the winner in a 2-1 away win at Swansea. QPR strode through the rounds and hammered Birmingham 7-2 on aggregate in the semis, Keen scoring in the 3-1 home leg win.

The first League Cup final to be played at Wembley saw 97,952 witness the historic win. Mike Keen was a skilled passer of the ball but also had great physicality and was terrific in the air.

To this day, he remains the only QPR captain to lead the R's to victory in a cup final!

GERRY FRANCIS

GERRY Francis could be described as QPR's most famous and ultimate captain as he not only captained the side during its most successful season in the top-flight, but also during the exciting Euro campaign the following year.

Added to this, Gerry captained England eight times, gaining 12 full caps between 1974 and 1976.

Francis had made his first-team debut against Liverpool in 1969 and it was also the famous Merseyside club that were on the receiving end of Gerry's 'goal of the season' in an opening-day 2-0 victory for the R's in that famous season of '75/76. He came through the ranks at Loftus Road and his first spell at the club was from 1968-1979, during which he made 295 appearances and scored 53 goals.

His career was later blighted by a back injury and when Gerry returned to QPR from Crystal Palace in 1981 he only managed 17 appearances, netting four times, before he left for Coventry in 1982.

The QPR captain had 'everything in his locker'. He was a born leader, strong tackler, had great vision and knew how to score goals . He also developed an almost-telepathic understanding with QPR star Stan Bowles as Rangers took the top-flight by storm in the mid-seventies.

The marauding midfielder, and a born leader of men, later took over the west

London club as manager in 1991 and in 1992/93 guided the R's to fifth place in the Premier League, finishing as London's top club.

The following season, we managed ninth and then eighth the campaign after. Gerry then left for Spurs but came back to QPR in 1998 to lead them out of trouble as the team had slumped into the lower end of what is now the Championship. He kept the R's out of trouble for two seasons before resigning.

He briefly became director of football before leaving in 2001 – but no-one can deny the impact and leadership of arguably QPR's greatest captain.

23

GLENN ROEDER

GLENN Roeder joined QPR from Leyton Orient in 1978 for £250,000 and made 157 appearances, netting 17 times, before joining Newcastle United in 1983. Glenn also gained six caps for England B while at QPR and it comes as no surprise as the elegant defender had it all.

The legendary R's number six was probably most famous though for the 'Roeder double shuffle' – a sort of smooth, double stepover which he had learned as a child and perfected in his time in west London.

The elegant centre-half was as comfortable on the ball going forward as even the most attack-minded players, and he would often produce the magic shuffle to get himself out of trouble in defence or to help mount another sweeping Rangers attack.

The continental style of play of that classic QPR team of the early eighties under manager and R's legend Terry Venables suited the graceful, forward-thinking defender Roeder down to the ground.

He became club captain during one of the club's most-successful and exciting spells, leading the Super Hoops to the FA Cup final against Tottenham but agonisingly missing the replay due to suspension – the R's losing narrowly 1-0 to a Glenn Hoddle penalty.

The following season, Glenn also led the team to the Second Division title and top-flight football once again before being transferred to Newcastle later that year.

RAY WILKINS

RAY Wilkins joined QPR from Scottish giants Glasgow Rangers in 1989 and at the age of 33, you could have been forgiven for thinking that his best years may have been behind him.

Think again!

The former Chelsea star had gone on to have a glittering career at the heart of midfield for Manchester United, AC Milan and Paris Saint-Germain before his move north of the border to Rangers and back south to west London.

His class, quality, influence and experience were apparent from day one and he was an integral part of a very successful, top-flight QPR side until he departed in 1994 for Crystal Palace.

Wilkins' stint at QPR was the longest in his football career and he was a regular during his time with the R's, including the club's first two seasons in the Premier League. The former England international and captain (84 full caps and three goals) appeared 154 times, scoring seven times between 1989 and 1994 and was instrumental in the free-flowing and free-scoring side that were ever-present at the top end of the top-flight of English football.

Ray left QPR to join Palace in 1994 but managed only one appearance for the Eagles (after breaking his foot).

'Super Ray' was brought back to W12 as player-manager following the exit of Gerry Francis and made a further 21 appearances during a two-year stint.

QUIZ

1. **In what position did QPR finish the 20/21 season?**

   peter Hucker

2. **Who finished the season as the R's top scorer?**

   Glenn Roeder

3. **How many did he notch in all competitions?**

   Tony Currie

4. **Which player made the most Championship appearances?**

   Middlesbrough and Blackpool

5. **Who started the season as squad number 13?**

   7

6. **Who scored for QPR in the season opener at home to Nottingham Forest?**

7. **What was unusual about the R's kit in the home fixture v Cardiff in October?**

8. **How many wins did the Hoops manage in the league campaign?**

9. **How many goals did the R's score in the League in the 20/21 campaign?**

10. **What was the overall goal difference for the season?**

11. Name the four players that joined in the January transfer window on loan?

12. Who took squad number 45?

13. The Super Hoops came from 2-0 down to win 3-2 at home to which club in March 2021?

14. Which team knocked QPR out of the FA Cup in January 2021?

15. Which player's thunder strike was voted goal of the season?

16. How many clean sheets did QPR keepers Seny Dieng and Joe Lumley keep between them?

17. Name the three players that received their marching orders during the campaign?

18. Which player was club captain this season?

19. Two players scored eight Championship goals each – can you name them?

20. QPR played two home games in front of fans in December – can you name the opponents?

Answers on page 60-61

SPOT THE DIFFERENCE

Can you spot the ten differences between these photos when QPR took on Millwall in August?

WORDSEARCH

Find the words in the grid. Words can go horizontally,
vertically and diagonally in all eight directions

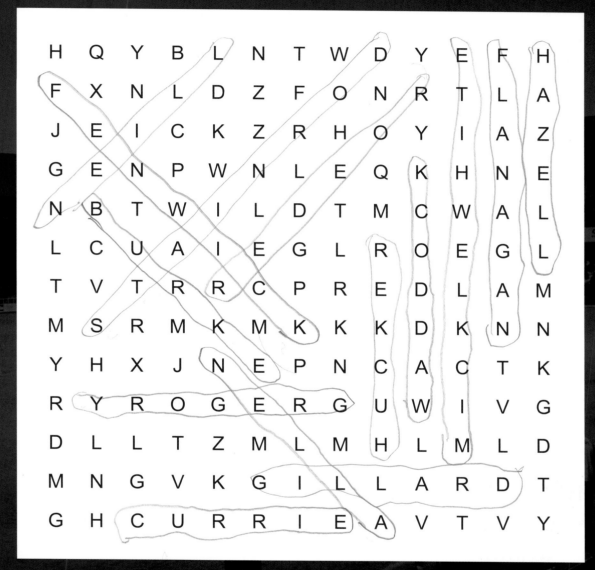

```
H  Q  Y  B  L  N  T  W  D  Y  E  F  H
F  X  N  L  D  Z  F  O  N  R  T  L  A
J  E  I  C  K  Z  R  H  O  Y  I  A  Z
G  E  N  P  W  N  L  E  Q  K  H  N  E
N  B  T  W  I  L  D  T  M  C  W  A  L
L  C  U  A  I  E  G  L  R  O  E  G  L
T  V  T  R  R  C  P  R  E  D  L  A  M
M  S  R  M  K  M  K  K  K  D  K  N  N
Y  H  X  J  N  E  P  N  C  A  C  T  K
R  Y  R  O  G  E  R  G  U  W  I  V  G
D  L  L  T  Z  M  L  M  H  L  M  L  D
M  N  G  V  K  G  I  L  L  A  R  D  T
G  H  C  U  R  R  I  E  A  V  T  V  Y
```

ALLEN	GILLARD	NEILL
BURKE	GREGORY	ROEDER
CURRIE	HAZELL	STAINROD
FENWICK	HUCKER	WADDOCK
FLANAGAN	MICKLEWHITE	

Answers on page 60-61

29

SAM **FIELD**

PLAYER OF THE YEAR: DICKIE SCOOPS AWARDS TREBLE

ROB Dickie was named as QPR's Sportito Supporters' Player of the Year for the 2020/21 campaign, pipping Seny Dieng to the top gong.

Following an extremely impressive first year at Championship level, the 25-year-old scooped three separate awards following the end-of-season vote.

Dickie shared the Ray Jones Players' Player of the Year award with the also-outstanding Dieng, while fans deemed that Rob's blockbuster attempt at Middlesbrough in April was worthy of the Kiyan Prince Goal of the Season accolade, too.

Elsewhere, Ilias Chair also picked up two personal awards as both the Daphne Biggs Young Player of the Year and Junior Hoops Player of the Year for 2020/21.

Finally, in what was a season like no other, there were two very worthy recipients of our Supporter of the Year award.

James Doe has long been an advocate of QPR in the Community Trust. This year, he led the QPR Race Europe team and ran a marathon the night before the event ended to gain top spot and raise vital funds for the Trust. James also virtually covered the distance of all 92 English league clubs, again raising money for our charitable arm.

James shared the award with the admirably-brave Luke Webber. Young Luke has been undergoing treatment for a brain tumour in the last 12 months but has shown incredible courage in the face of adversity and plenty of continued support for his favourite team, too.

Many congratulations to all our winners.

SPORTITO SUPPORTERS' PLAYER OF THE YEAR
ROB DICKIE

SPORTITO SUPPORTERS' PLAYER OF THE YEAR:
Rob Dickie (40% of vote)
Runner-up: Seny Dieng (35%)

ILIAS CHAIR

JAMES DOE
AND
LUKE WEBBER

JUNIOR HOOPS PLAYER OF THE YEAR:
Ilias Chair
Runner-up: Rob Dickie

SUPPORTER(S) OF THE YEAR:
James Doe & Luke Webber

ROB DICKIE

ILIAS CHAIR

KIYAN PRINCE GOAL OF THE SEASON:
Rob Dickie v Middlesbrough A **(46%)**
Runner-up: Dom Ball v Cardiff City
(36%)

DAPHNE BIGGS SUPPORTERS' YOUNG PLAYER OF THE YEAR:
Ilias Chair **(60%)**
Runner-up: Chris Willock **(36%)**

PLAYER
OF THE YEAR
AWARDS
2020/21

DICKIE
& DIENG

RAY JONES PLAYERS'
PLAYER OF THE YEAR

RAY
JONES
PLAYERS'
PLAYER(S)
OF THE
YEAR:
Rob Dickie
& Seny
Dieng

OFFICIAL 2021/22
QPR HOME KIT

AVAILABLE IN STORE & ONLINE

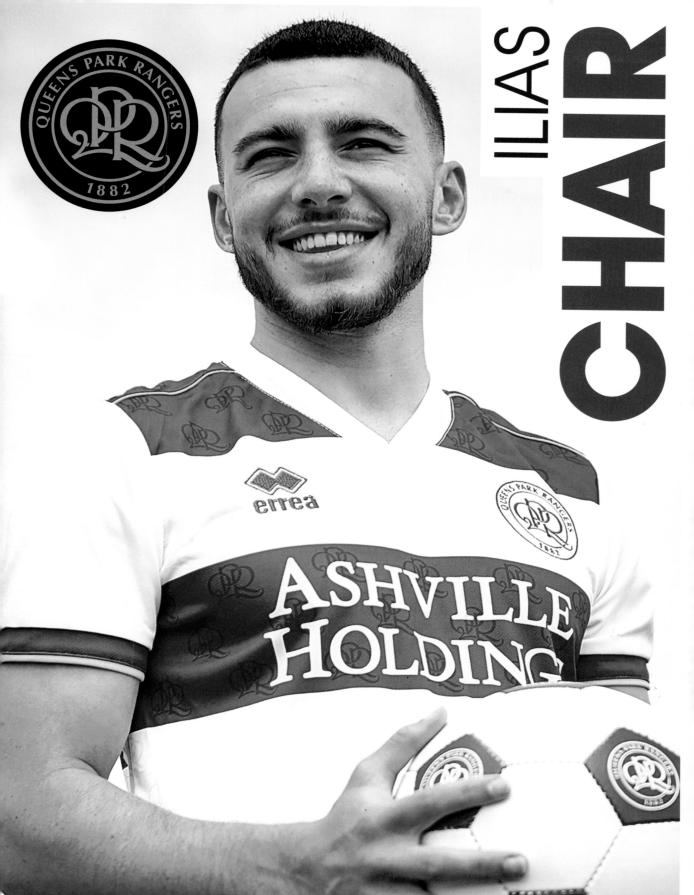

ILIAS CHAIR

FOCUS ON...

LEE WALLACE

MARRIED: Yes

CHILDREN: Four

FAVOURITE TV PROGRAMME: Monday Night Football, Sky Sports

FAVOURITE PLAYER (WORLD FOOTBALL): Lionel Messi

MOST PROMISING TEAM-MATE: Ilias Chair or Chrissy Willock

FAVOURITE 'OTHER' TEAM: Glasgow Rangers

CHILDHOOD FOOTBALLING HERO: Ronaldo (R9)

FAVOURITE OTHER SPORT: Boxing

MOST DIFFICULT OPPONENT (PLAYER) SO FAR: Zlatan Ibrahimović

MOST MEMORABLE MATCH: Old Firm derbies in 2012 and 2015.

BIGGEST DISAPPOINTMENT IN FOOTBALL: Final loss with Glasgow Rangers in 2015.

FAVOURITE MEAL: Pizza

FAVOURITE HOLIDAY DESTINATION: Florida

FAVOURITE ACTIVITY ON DAY OFF: Going for a coffee and a walk.

POST-MATCH ROUTINE: Home, think and talk about the match with family, eat, watch football.

BEST FRIEND(S) IN FOOTBALL: Too many to name (Dom Ball at QPR)!

BIGGEST CAREER INFLUENCE: Parents

PERSONAL AMBITION: Finish career having positively impacted as many team-mates as possible, on and off pitch.

IF YOU WEREN'T A FOOTBALLER, WHAT WOULD YOU BE: Too difficult to answer!

PERSON IN WORLD YOU'D MOST LIKE TO MEET: Pep Guardiola

JORDY
DE WIJS

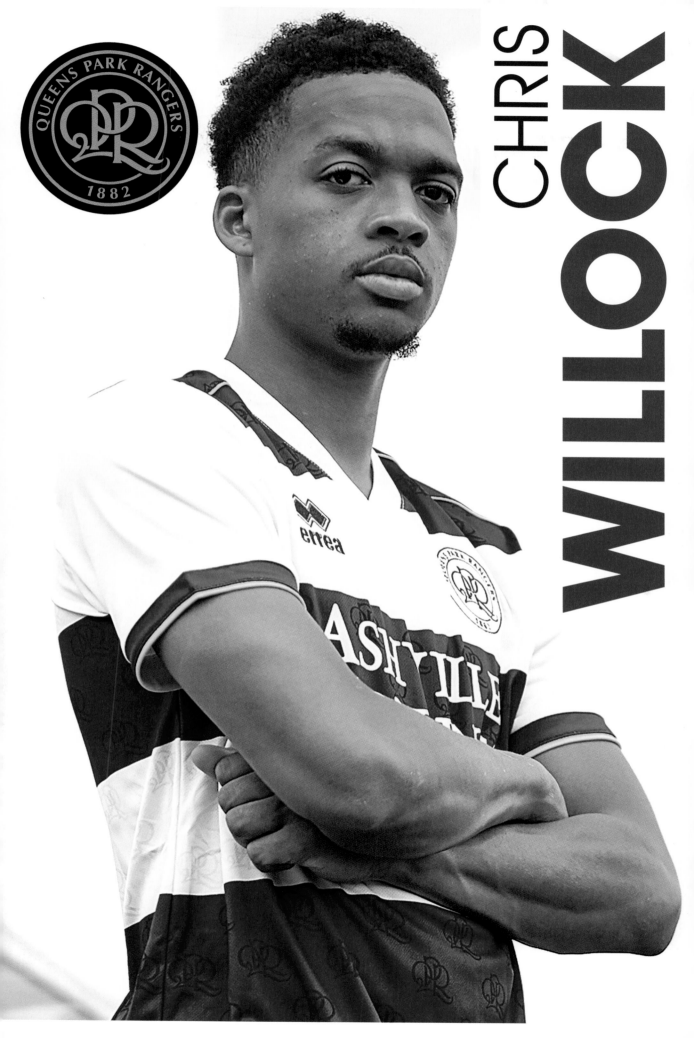

QUEENS PARK RANGERS
1882

CHRIS WILLOCK

GOAL RUSH!

THE 2020/21 season was another campaign full of blockbuster efforts from the R's.

Once again, we whittle down the pick of the bunch and also reveal the goal of the season, as voted for by you – the QPR fans!

TODD KANE
V CARDIFF (H)

Rangers then doubled their lead with less than half an hour on the clock. On 27 minutes, Chair turned provider – his low centre from the left was deflected into the path of Todd Kane and the full-back volleyed the ball into the top corner from 16 yards. Smart finish!

ILIAS CHAIR
V CARDIFF (H)

The first of three goal-of-the-season contenders in exactly the same fixture! Rangers beat the Bluebirds 3-2 in a topsy-turvy W12 fixture in late October 2020. R's pressure paid off with the opening goal in the 15th minute when the impressive Albert Adomah stood a delivery up to the far post for Chair, who waited patiently for the ball to drop before volleying into the ground and over helpless former QPR custodian Alex Smithies.

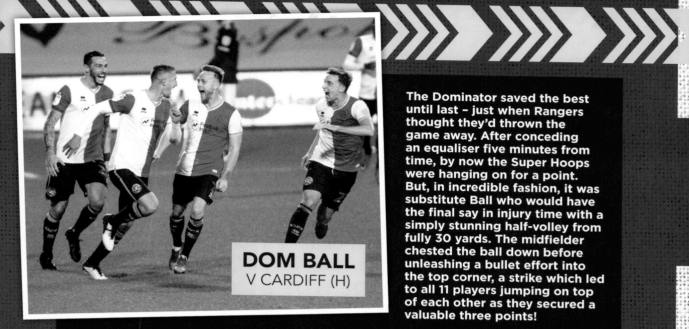

The Dominator saved the best until last – just when Rangers thought they'd thrown the game away. After conceding an equaliser five minutes from time, by now the Super Hoops were hanging on for a point. But, in incredible fashion, it was substitute Ball who would have the final say in injury time with a simply stunning half-volley from fully 30 yards. The midfielder chested the ball down before unleashing a bullet effort into the top corner, a strike which led to all 11 players jumping on top of each other as they secured a valuable three points!

DOM BALL
V CARDIFF (H)

BRIGHT OSAYI-SAMUEL
V ROTHERHAM (H)

The R's secured another nail-biting, 3-2 victory over the Millers in November. Bright made it 2-1 to QPR on the stroke of half-time. After being denied previously, Osayi-Samuel played a neat one-two with Geoff Cameron before once again striding into the penalty area. This time, though, he fired beyond Jamal Blackman to hand Rangers the initiative once more.

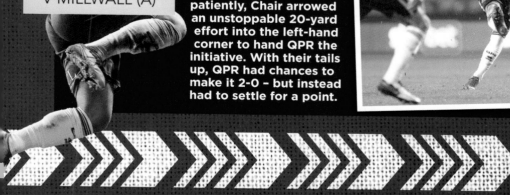

ILIAS CHAIR
V MILLWALL (A)

Rangers played out a 1-1 draw at The Den in December, but Chair's opener was worthy of being the match-winner. Rangers then took the lead on 53 minutes. After Mark Warburton's men built patiently, Chair arrowed an unstoppable 20-yard effort into the left-hand corner to hand QPR the initiative. With their tails up, QPR had chances to make it 2-0 – but instead had to settle for a point.

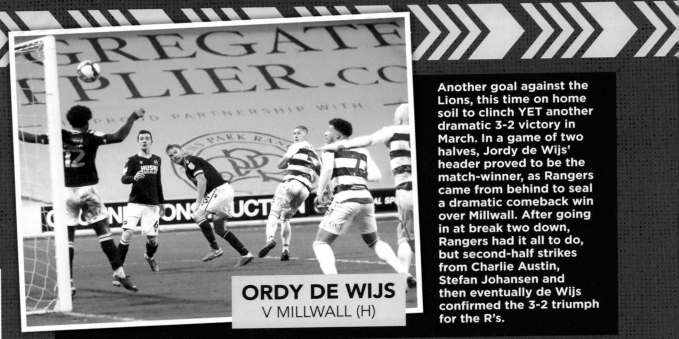

ORDY DE WIJS
V MILLWALL (H)

Another goal against the Lions, this time on home soil to clinch YET another dramatic 3-2 victory in March. In a game of two halves, Jordy de Wijs' header proved to be the match-winner, as Rangers came from behind to seal a dramatic comeback win over Millwall. After going in at break two down, Rangers had it all to do, but second-half strikes from Charlie Austin, Stefan Johansen and then eventually de Wijs confirmed the 3-2 triumph for the R's.

LYNDON DYKES
V READING (A)

The January arrival of Charlie Austin coincided with a real upturn in form for Scotland number nine Lyndon Dykes. Rangers drew 1-1 at Reading in March. Dykes netted just before half-time after a brilliant team move involving Ilias Chair and Lee Wallace, but that advantage was quickly lost after the restart when Yakou Meite beat Seny Dieng from close range.

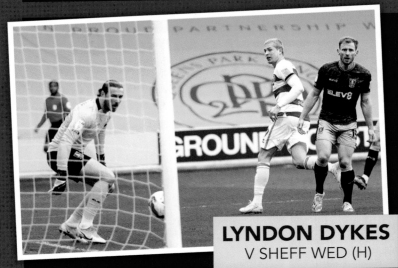

LYNDON DYKES
V SHEFF WED (H)

Dykes bagged a double at home to Sheffield Wednesday in April – with his first goal particularly impressive. The hosts took the lead on 27 minutes with a stunning effort from Lyndon. Yoann Barbet picked the Scotland striker out with a perfect delivery from the left. Dykes still had plenty to do but he managed to beat Joe Wildsmith with a downward header from 16 yards for his eighth goal of the season.

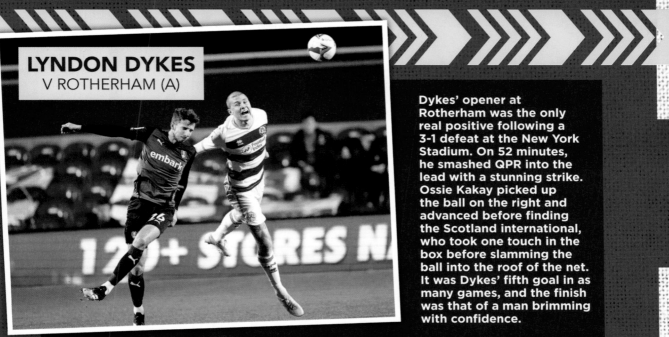

LYNDON DYKES
V ROTHERHAM (A)

Dykes' opener at Rotherham was the only real positive following a 3-1 defeat at the New York Stadium. On 52 minutes, he smashed QPR into the lead with a stunning strike. Ossie Kakay picked up the ball on the right and advanced before finding the Scotland international, who took one touch in the box before slamming the ball into the roof of the net. It was Dykes' fifth goal in as many games, and the finish was that of a man brimming with confidence.

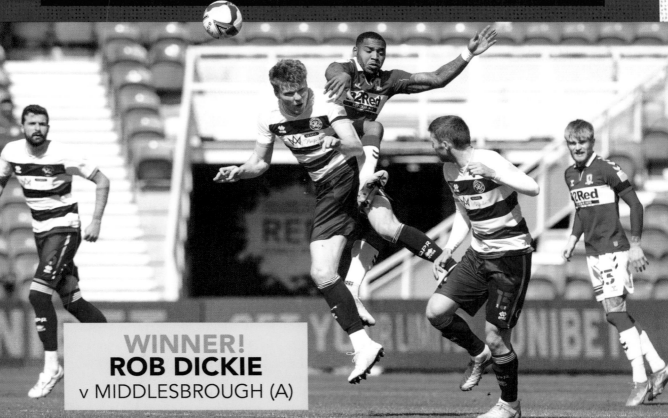

WINNER!
ROB DICKIE
v MIDDLESBROUGH (A)

Worthy winner. A superb first 20 minutes from Rangers was enough to secure a 2-1 victory at the Riverside Stadium in April, despite being reduced to 10 men. Rob Dickie gave the R's the lead with a fantastic 30-yard effort, before Lee Wallace doubled Rangers' advantage minutes later. Midway through the second half, with Boro already having pulled a goal back, Seny Dieng was shown his marching orders for a late tackle on Duncan Watmore, meaning Mark Warburton's side had half an hour to play with 10 men. But Rangers dug in deep and were able to leave Teesside with the victory.

CUP QUIZ: '82 Relived

THIS season marks 40 years since QPR made it to the 1982 FA Cup final to face Tottenham Hotspur, in a campaign still fondly remembered by R's fans.

But how is your R's knowledge when it comes to that particular year?
Test yourself...

1 Name the QPR goalkeeper for the 1982 cup final and replay?

2 Which outfield player captained the side in that first final, only to miss out through suspension for the replay?

3 Which R's player took over the captaincy for the replay?

4 In both round three and round four of the cup in 1982, QPR had been taken to a replay on their way to Wembley. Can you name both teams? One point for each.

5 Clive Allen was the club's top goalscorer, but how many did he notch on the way to the final - 6,7 or 8?

CUP QUIZ: '82 *Relived*

>>>

6 Who scored the decisive goal in both the quarter-final and semi-final wins?

7 Who were the opponents who were narrowly beaten at a packed Loftus Road in the quarter-finals?

8 Who was the QPR stalwart that played his last game for the club in the final replay?

9 Which two players for QPR were involved in the build-up to the equalising goal at Wembley? One point for each.

10 In which minute did that equaliser come?

11 One QPR player was very unfortunate in that the ball deflected off him for the first Spurs goal in the first match, and he also gave away a penalty in the replay. Name him.

12 At which stadium was the semi-final played?

13 QPR were hit by an injury in the final to top scorer Clive Allen after only a couple of minutes, he played on but was eventually substituted after 50 minutes. Who replaced him?

14 What was unusual about the strips that both Spurs and QPR wore in the final?

15 The combined crowd for the two matches was over 190,000. True or false?

16 Who was the manager of the west London club at the time?

17 Who was the player who came on as a substitute for Rangers in the replay? Was it A. Wayne Fereday, B. Ian Stewart or C. Steve Burke?

18 Clive Alen scored four goals in one match during the cup run, against which opponents?

19 Name the QPR player who hit the bar in the replay?

20 Which QPR defender remains the only player ever to score for the R's in an FA Cup final?

Answers on page 60-61

ANDRE **DOZZELL**

ALBERT **ADOMAH**

LYNDON DYKES

MARRIED: Yes

CHILDREN: Yes

CAR: Golf GTI

FAVOURITE TV PROGRAMME: Friends

FAVOURITE PLAYER (WORLD FOOTBALL): Zlatan Ibrahimović

MOST PROMISING TEAM-MATE: Chris Willock

FAVOURITE 'OTHER' TEAM: Livingston and Queen of the South

CHILDHOOD FOOTBALLING HERO: Didier Drogba

FAVOURITE OTHER SPORT: When I was younger I would say rugby league but I like doing pretty much all sports.

MOST DIFFICULT OPPONENT (PLAYER) SO FAR: Luka Modrić

MOST MEMORABLE MATCH: Scotland v Serbia to qualify for the Euros.

BIGGEST DISAPPOINTMENT IN FOOTBALL: I don't know, I would say it's been amazing so far.

FAVOURITE MEAL: It's hard to say one.

FAVOURITE HOLIDAY DESTINATION: Cyprus

FAVOURITE PERSONALITY: Kevin Hart

FAVOURITE ACTIVITY ON DAY OFF: Just spending some time at home with the family or golf.

FAVOURITE MUSICIAN / BAND: Hard to pick one there are so many. The Game has to be up there.

POST-MATCH ROUTINE: Just go home, usually get a takeaway and chill out.

BEST FRIEND(S) IN FOOTBALL: I have a couple back in Scotland that I always keep in touch with.

PERSONAL AMBITION: To play in the Premier League.

IF YOU WEREN'T A FOOTBALLER, WHAT WOULD YOU BE: No clue, probably working in a factory somewhere!

PERSON IN WORLD YOU'D MOST LIKE TO MEET: The Rock

2021/22 QPR HOME

INTRODUCING YOUR
2021/22 QPR KITS!

QPR'S new kits for the 2021/22 season landed in July!

2021/22 QPR HOME

Inspired by the 1991/92 Brooks kit - a fan favourite - our new home shirt features a fluorescent yellow trim on the shoulders and sleeve, and a crest watermark subtly featured within the hoops.

The away kit also carries this subtle watermark, sporting black and charcoal hoops and is topped off with fine gold piping. The shorts and socks are also black.

The home and away shirts have been made using Errea's new and revolutionary Ti-Energy fabric, which has antiviral and antibacterial properties along with Minusnine J1+ treatment which repels liquids and droplets.

This means the Ti-Energy shirts offer the perfect combination of maximum performance and increased safety for all players and fans of QPR.

QPR boss Mark Warburton told us; "The kits look great and I am sure the fans will enjoy the tie-in to the 1991/92 season, which was a successful period for the club in the top-flight.

"We know the history of a football club is so important but we also need to make sure we work hard to create new memorable moments for the fans."

Fabrizio Taddei, Errea head of pro clubs department, said: "Once again, we have worked closely with the club to produce a traditional home shirt with some eye-catching extra details, not least the tonal effect in the hoops.

"The black and gold away shirt is simply stunning and something we are particularly proud to have produced."

2021/22 **QPR AWAY**

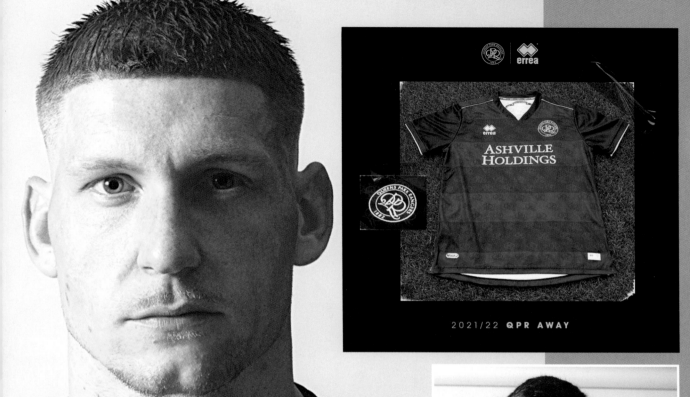

2021/22 **QPR AWAY**

The 2021/22 replica kits are available to purchase from the Stadium Superstore and online, at shop.qpr.co.uk.

OFFICIAL 2021/22 QPR AWAY KIT

AVAILABLE IN STORE & ONLINE

ROB **DICKIE**

ASHVILLE HOLDINGS

OSSIE KAKAY

MARRIED: Not yet!

CHILDREN: One, three-year-old son

CAR: Mercedes

FAVOURITE TV PROGRAMME: EastEnders!

FAVOURITE PLAYER (WORLD FOOTBALL): Cristiano Ronaldo

MOST PROMISING TEAM-MATE: Chris Willock

FAVOURITE 'OTHER' TEAM: Man United

CHILDHOOD FOOTBALLING HERO: Andy Cole

FAVOURITE OTHER SPORT: Tennis

MOST MEMORABLE MATCH: Stoke away last season - scoring my first Championship goal.

BIGGEST DISAPPOINTMENT IN FOOTBALL: The injuries so far.

FAVOURITE MEAL: Jollof rice

FAVOURITE HOLIDAY DESTINATION: Greece

FAVOURITE ACTIVITY ON DAY OFF: Swimming or going to the gym.

FAVOURITE MUSICIAN / BAND: Lil Durk

POST-MATCH ROUTINE: Eat a nice meal and watch a movie!

BEST FRIEND(S) IN FOOTBALL: Niko Hämäläinen & Mide Shodipo

BIGGEST CAREER INFLUENCE: Definitely my family.

PERSONAL AMBITION: To play at the highest level possible.

IF YOU WEREN'T A FOOTBALLER, WHAT WOULD YOU BE: A PE teacher!

ANSWERS

PAGE 26/27 **QUIZ**

1. 9
2. Lyndon Dykes
3. 12
4. Yoann Barbet with 46
5. Seny Dieng
6. Lyndon Dykes and Ilias Chair
7. QPR wore a one-off red and white halved kit
8. 19
9. 57
10. +2
11. Jordi de Wijs, Sam Field, Stefan Johansen and Charlie Austin
12. Charlie Austin
13. Millwall
14. Fulham
15. Rob Dickie
16. 14
17. Rob Dickie, Todd Kane and Seny Dieng
18. Geoff Cameron
19. Ilias Chair and Charlie Austin
20. Reading and Stoke

PAGE 28 **SPOT THE DIFFERENCE**

PAGE 29 **WORDSEARCH**

```
H Q Y B L N T W D Y E F H
F X N L D Z F O N R T L A
J E I C K Z R H O Y I A Z
G E N P W N L E Q K H N E
N B T W I L D T M C W A L
L C U A I E G L R O E G L
T V T R R C P R E D L A M
M S R M K M K K K D K N N
Y H X J N E P N C A C T K
R Y R O G E R G U W I V G
D L L T Z M L M H L M L D
M N G V K G I L L A R D T
G H C U R R I E A V T V Y
```

Pages 44-47 **CUP QUIZ**

1. Peter Hucker
2. Glenn Roeder
3. Tony Currie
4. Middlesbrough and Blackpool
5. 7
6. Clive Allen
7. Crystal Palace
8. Ian Gillard
9. Simon Stainrod and Bob Hazell
10. 115th minute (extra-time)
11. Tony Currie
12. Highbury, then home of Arsenal
13. Gary Micklewhite
14. They both wore away kits, even though there was no clash between QPR's home and Spurs' away, or vice versa.
15. True
16. Terry Venables
17. C. Steve Burke
18. Blackpool
19. John Gregory
20. Terry Fenwick

SKY BET CHAMPIONSHIP
FIXTURES 2021/22

DATE	OPPONENTS	H/A	ACTUAL SCORE
SAT AUG 7	MILLWALL	H	
SAT AUG 14	HULL CITY	A	
WED AUG 18	MIDDLESBROUGH	A	
SAT AUG 21	BARNSLEY	H	
SAT AUG 28	COVENTRY	H	
SAT SEP 11	READING	A	
TUE SEP 14	BOURNEMOUTH	A	
SAT SEP 18	BRISTOL CITY	H	
FRI SEP 24	WEST BROM	A	
TUE SEP 28	BIRMINGHAM	H	
SAT OCT 2	PRESTON	H	
SAT OCT 16	FULHAM	A	
TUE OCT 19	BLACKBURN	H	
SAT OCT 23	PETERBOROUGH	A	
FRI OCT 29	NOTT'M FOREST	H	
WED NOV 3	CARDIFF	A	
SAT NOV 6	BLACKPOOL	A	
SAT NOV 20	LUTON TOWN	H	
WED NOV 24	HUDDERSFIELD	H	
SAT NOV 27	DERBY	A	
SAT DEC 4	STOKE CITY	H	
SAT DEC 11	SHEFFIELD UTD	A	
SAT DEC 18	SWANSEA	H	
SUN DEC 26	BOURNEMOUTH	H	
WED DEC 29	BRISTOL CITY	A	